PLANTS

Wetland Plants

Ernestine Giesecke

Heinemann Library
Des Plaines, Illinois

Designed by Depke Design
Illustrations by Eileen Mueller Neill
Printed in Hong Kong

03 02 01 00 99
10 9 8 7 6 5 4 3 2 1

Library of Congress Cataloging-in-Publication Data

Giesecke, Ernestine, 1945-
    Wetland plants / Ernestine Giesecke.
      p. cm. – (Plants)
    Includes bibliographical references (p.   ) and index.
    Summary: Describes how various plants adapt to life in wetlands, including the Venus fly trap, sphagnum moss, and cranberry.
    ISBN 1-57572-830-3 (lib. bdg.)
    1. Wetland plants—Juvenile literature. [1. Wetland plants.]
I. Title. II. Series: Plants (Des Plaines, Ill.)
QK938.M3G54   1999
581.768—dc21   98-44524
                                                                CIP
                                                                AC

Acknowledgments:

The Publisher would like to thanks the following for permission to reproduce photographs:
Cover: Michael Gadomski/Earth Scenes
Michael Gadomski/Earth Scenes p. 4; Richard Shell/Earth Scenes p. 5; Ted Levin/Earth Scenes p. 8; Patti Murray/Earth Scenes p. 9; Terry G. Murphy/Earth Scenes pp. 10-11; Maria Zorn/Earth Scenes p. 12; Dr. E.R. Degginger pp. 14-16, 22-23; Jerome Wexler/Photo Researchers p. 17; Dr. E.R. Degginger/Earth Scenes pp. 18, 24, 27; John Lemker/Earth Scenes p. 20; Anne Heimann pp. 21, 29; Phil Degginger/Dr. E.R. Degginger p. 25; B.G. Murray/Earth Scenes p. 26; Jeff Lepore/Photo Researchers p. 28.

Some words are shown in bold, **like this.** You can find out what they mean by looking in the glossary.

CAUTION!
Always take an adult with you when you visit wetlands. Be careful where you step—the ground is often soft and soggy!

Contents

The Wetlands

Wetland **soils** are usually soggy. Wetland areas are often flooded. There are three kinds of wetlands—marsh, swamp, and bog. This is a picture of a marsh. It is an area of spongy, wet ground with pools of still water.

A swamp is land covered in still or slowly
moving water. This is a picture of a bog.
It is a damp, spongy place. The bottom of
a bog is usually lined with **peat**.

Wetland Plants

Jewel Weed

Venus Fly Trap

Jack-in-the-Pulpit

Marsh Marigold

Hooded
Pitcher Plant

Sphagnum Moss

Different plants grow in different kinds of
wetlands. Yet in each wetland there are
plants, like grasses and cattails, that grow
partly in and partly out of the water.

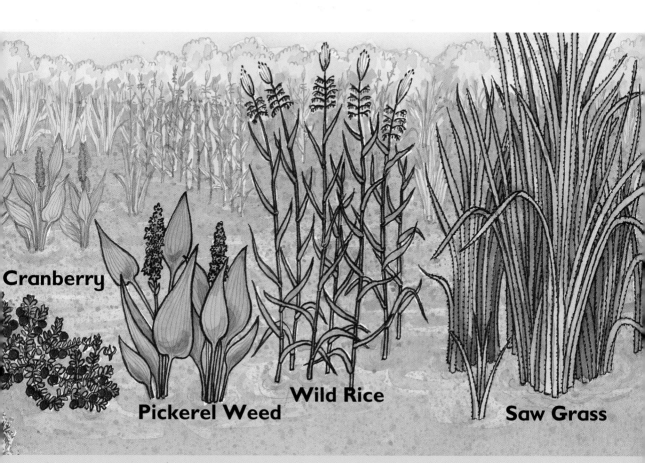

Cranberry

Pickerel Weed

Wild Rice

Saw Grass

Wetlands also have plants that float on the surface of the water. There are even plants that live entirely under the water.

Saw Grass

Saw grass is an important part of a marsh. It has strong underground stems and roots. These stems and roots hold the **soil** and keep it from washing away during storms.

These kinds of grasses may burn in dry weather. But new plants grow from the underground stems. Marsh grasses provide homes for many kinds of birds.

Wild Rice

Wild rice is a type of grass that grows in marshy areas. It is an **annual** plant. That means at the end of the season the old plants die. New plants grow from seeds each year.

Wild rice is an important food **crop** in some parts of the country. The rice grains are the seeds of the plant. The seeds are **harvested** from the growing plants. Then the seeds are packaged and sold.

Marsh Marigold

The marsh marigold can be found in
mountain areas. It often grows in the wet,
soggy ground near the edge of snow banks.

The marsh marigold has leaves at the bottom of the plant. Its flower stands on top of a stem without leaves.

Venus Fly Trap

The venus fly trap is a **carnivorous**, or meat-eating plant. The plant gets the **nutrients** it needs by trapping insects and spiders in its leaves.

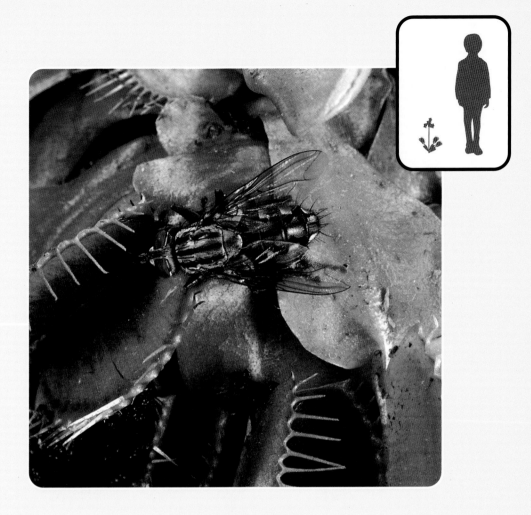

Each leaf has two halves. Each half is lined with hairs. When an insect disturbs the hairs, the plant snaps shut. Once the insect is trapped, the plant produces juices that begin to **digest** the insect.

Jack-in-the-Pulpit

The jack-in-the-pulpit flower hides under a long thin leaf. The plant has a large underground **tuber** that helps it stay in place in a swamp.

In late summer and early fall, the plant produces red berries. The berries provide food for many kinds of birds and small animals.

Pickerel Weed

Pickerel weed grows in the shallow, quiet water found in some swamps. It has a creeping underground stem. Its violet blue flower appears above the water.

The plant has nut-like seeds that are
eaten by birds and other animals. Deer
often feed on the plant's young stalks.

Jewel Weed

The jewel weed is an **annual** plant that
lives in swampy areas. It produces bright
yellow and orange flowers. These provide
food for hummingbirds, bees, and ants.

The plant is also called a touch-me-not.
Any **slight** brush against the plant's seed
pods makes the seeds fly out in all
directions.

Sphagnum Moss

Sphagnum (SFAG-num) moss is one of the many mosses that lives in bogs. Like all mosses, it does not have roots. It soaks up the **nutrients** it needs from the water around it.

The leaves of sphagnum moss take in water. The plant is like a sponge. It can hold twenty times its weight in water!

Cranberry

Another bog plant is the cranberry. The cranberry plant is an **evergreen**. Its leaves stay green all year long, even through fall and winter.

The cranberry is the fruit of the plant. It floats on water. The plant is grown and **harvested** as a food **crop** in states such as Washington, New Jersey, Massachusetts, Oregon, and Wisconsin.

Hooded Pitcher Plant

The hooded pitcher plant is a **carnivorous** plant that lives in bogs. The plant produces a honey-like liquid that attracts insects.

Once the insect enters the plant, it is trapped by the downward-pointing hairs. The insect drowns in the water at the bottom of the plant. Then the plant **digests** the insect.

Wetlands Today

For many years, people did not see how important it was that wetlands supported many different kinds of plants. The plants provided food and homes for many kinds of birds and other animals.

Today, people are working to save wetland **habitats**. In some cases, they are rebuilding the wetlands like in this picture. In some places, **migrating** birds have returned to the wetland areas.

Glossary

annual a plant that lives its entire life in one year

crop a plant grown for food or money

carnivorous feeds on animals

digest change food to obtain its nutrients

evergreen plant whose leaves stay green and functional all year long

habitats place where a plant or animal normally lives

harvested gathered in a **crop**

migrating moving from one place to another

nutrients things plants need to grow

peat dead and rotting plant material

slight small

soil the ground plants grow in

tubers thick underground part of some plants

Parts of a Plant

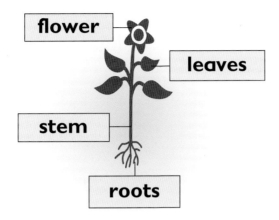

More Books to Read

Amsel, Sheri. *A Wetland Walk*. Brookfield, CT: Millbrook Press, Inc. 1993.

Dunphy, Madeleine. *Here Is the Wetland*. New York: Hyperion Books for Children. 1996.

Fowler, Allan. *Life In a Wetland*. Danbury, CT: Franklin Watts. 1998.

Gibbons, Gail. *Marshes & Swamps*. New York: Holiday House, Inc. 1998.

Staub, Frank. *America's Wetlands*. Minneapolis, MN: Lerner Publishing Group 1994.

Stone, Lynn M. *Wetlands*. Vero Beach, FL: Rourke Corporation. 1996.

Index